This book is published strictly for historical purposes.
The Naval and Military Press Ltd
expressly bears no responsibility or liability of any type,
to any first, second or third party, for any harm,
injury or loss whatsoever.

# BALL-PUNCHING

Pivot Punch on Double-ended Ball

*Frontispiece*]

# BALL-PUNCHING

BY

TOM CARPENTER

World's Champion All-round Ball-Puncher

WITH EIGHTEEN ILLUSTRATIONS

The Naval & Military Press Ltd

*Published by*

# The Naval & Military Press Ltd
Unit 5 Riverside, Brambleside
Bellbrook Industrial Estate
Uckfield, East Sussex
TN22 1QQ England

Tel: +44 (0)1825 749494

www.naval-military-press.com
www.nmarchive.com

*In reprinting in facsimile from the original, any imperfections are inevitably reproduced and the quality may fall short of modern type and cartographic standards.*

# CONTENTS

| | PAGE |
|---|---|
| FOREWORD | 1 |
| APPARATUS, ETC. | 4 |
| PRELIMINARY EXERCISES | 11 |
| GETTING AND KEEPING FIT | 18 |
| BALL-PUNCHING FOR BOXERS | 31 |
| FANCY BALL-PUNCHING | 40 |
| THE DOUBLE-ENDED PUNCH-BALL | 62 |

# ILLUSTRATIONS

| | PAGE |
|---|---|
| Pivot Punch on Double-ended Ball | *Frontispiece* |
| Straight Left | 12 |
| Tattoo Punch | 15 |
| Cross Punch | 17 |
| Striking the Ball with the back of the Elbow | 20 |
| Striking the Ball backwards with the Fist | 22 |
| Striking the Ball with the Elbow behind the Body | 25 |
| Operating Floor Ball with the Feet | 29 |
| Half Uppercut | 36 |
| Right Swing | 37 |
| Striking the Ball with the Outside of the Elbow | 43 |
| Operating two Platform Balls Simultaneously | 45 |
| Cross Punch on the Wall Ball | 49 |
| Fist and Elbow Punch on the Floor Ball | 52 |
| Operating Three Floor Balls Simultaneously | 56 |
| Operating Four Balls Simultaneously | 59 |
| Operating Three Balls Simultaneously | 61 |
| Straight Left on Double-ended Ball | 65 |

# BALL-PUNCHING

## FOREWORD

Is there a boom in ball-punching ? No, not a boom, but a steadily increasing recognition of the advantages of this ideal exerciser. Let me enumerate a few. It brings into action every muscle of the body ; develops them in correct and natural proportions ; imparts a suppleness, which is the essence of graceful movement ; quickens the eye and stimulates the brain ; thus thinking and acting become practically simultaneous. The lungs are strengthened ; the breathing and other internal functions of the body regulated, and the circulation improved. Such benefits no ordinary muscle exerciser can possibly give. Then again, it has a mysterious fascination, so strong that no amount of repetition will make its use become monotonous. If you think for a moment you will see how really important this is, because any exercise which captures and holds your interest must do you far more good than one which does not—no amount of will-power can enable you to take a real interest in the performance of a merely mechanical repetition. It is not the kind of grinding task for health's sake that you force yourself into by a New Year's resolution and drop a few days afterwards. No, it is a pleasant daily exercise that you will look forward to all the year round. Small wonder then that it is gaining in popularity, and I am sure it will be more and more appreciated as these considerations become known.

At one time the swing type of ball was seldom found in use outside of the boxer's training quarters, but now I am receiving enquiries every day from athletes of all descriptions asking me to give them a course of exercises on this type of ball. There are also many who, through lack of time or some other reason, are unable to take an active part in athletics or outdoor sports, but, nevertheless, desire to keep fit. They find ball-punching the finest means by which to attain that energy and vitality so valuable in everyday life, whilst to sufferers from indigestion, malaise, flatulence, etc., I would especially recommend it as a less expensive and greatly preferable alternative to doctors' bills or artificial treatment.

Nor is it too strenuous for ladies or children.

The actual punching can be moderated to suit the occasion, without in any way interfering with the benefits to be derived. My pupils have included several ladies, who have become experts, carrying off prizes in open competitions against all comers, and my family of four boys and two girls are all well versed in the art, with a resultant " clean bill of health."

If you are looking for a healthy hobby, brimful of amusement and requiring no small amount of skill, let me commend you to fancy ball-punching. With constant practice you may bring it to a fine art, and give an exhibition which will fill your friends with admiration.

These, then, are the considerations which have prompted me to attempt this work, greater in its scope than any previously written on the subject, and I have endeavoured to describe the exercises in the clearest terms so that every reader may follow them with ease.

TOM CARPENTER

# APPARATUS, FIXING, AND GENERAL HINTS

## The Platform

To get the best results from the swing punch-ball, it is advisable to have a platform. By far the most popular pattern is that which fixes to the wall, because of its convenience and the moderate price at which one can be purchased. In fact, I claim that their introduction has done more to popularise the suspended ball than anything else. They are portable, easily fixed or removed, and can be folded out of the way when not in use. When selecting your platform, see that it is solidly built, otherwise the vibration will shake it to pieces. The drum should be round, not less than 2ft. in diameter, and of hard close-grained wood, smoothly finished, so as not to give the ball more wear than necessary. An adjustable platform has the advantage of being suitable for persons of various heights, and is essential in gymnasiums, clubs, etc., where many people use the ball. Fix it securely so that it is perfectly rigid, and in such a position that the drum is just a hand-spread above the head. Here I must warn you against having the ball too high, which is a very dangerous practice, and may lead to serious consequences. The four-poster stand as used by professional ball-punchers, boxers, etc., is, of course, preferable where serious work is contemplated and space permits. These are usually made to suit personal requirements. In fixing one of these, see that the uprights are screwed securely into the cross-pieces. The guy-wires should be crossed and fastened to the floor about 2ft. apart, but it is most important that they should not touch at the point of crossing.

THE BALL.

Now we come to the ball itself. Shape is the first consideration, for if it is not correct in this detail, it will jump and be very difficult to control. I have spent much time and thought experimenting on the subject, trying some hundreds of different makes and shapes. My very first attempt was made on a pigskin bladder filled with water, but when this burst, giving me an unexpected shower-bath, I decided that the air-inflated spheroid was more convenient to practise on. The difficulty at that time was to get something light, and at the same time strong, and after trying sailcloth and various other materials, I eventually made the ball for my first public exhibition from kid leather and lined it with a fine, strong canvas. The shape was the same as that in the accompanying illustrations, which is undoubtedly the most successful. It has since been universally approved, and has almost entirely displaced all other patterns. As regards weight, for fast work and fancy punching, the lightest ball possible should be procured, but it should be borne in mind that such a ball will not stand " slogging." For hard wear, such as is given in gymnasiums or for heavy training, a strong ball of the light hide type should be chosen. Boxers have, as a rule, at least two—a light one for quickness, and a heavy one on which to let themselves go all out. It is advisable to have a small leather loop at the top of the ball, then, should the cord break, it will not be necessary to deflate, as would be the case if the cord were passed directly through the top of the ball. The objection to such a loop has been that it prevented the ball from hanging truly, but I have just perfected an arrangement for passing the cord through the loop and thus both

## APPARATUS, FIXING, & GENERAL HINTS 7

advantages are maintained. Cotton cord, $\frac{3}{8}$in., is the best thing for fastening the ball to the swivel. Pigskin is strong, but apt to stretch. The length of the cord should be 3in. between loop and swivel, or, if the ball has no loop, 3$\frac{1}{2}$in. See that the knot inside the swivel is a small one, and has plenty of room to spin round, otherwise the cord will cockle up, and I have seen many otherwise good exhibitions spoiled by this. Also make sure that the fastenings are perfectly secure. Do not inflate the ball to its utmost. It is about right when a slight impression can be made by pressing with the little finger.

In practising the exercises on the floor-ball, bare boarding should be chosen where possible, as linoleum deadens the ball, making it slow in action. If it is inconvenient to screw the swivel to the floor, many of the exercises described in this book can be practised by fastening it to a batten of wood about 6in. long, and standing on this, one foot on each side of the swivel. Unless otherwise stated, the length of cord for the floor-ball should be about 6in.

Gymnasium boots or shoes should be worn whilst practising, the lighter the better, as quickness on the feet is most essential to good ball-punching. Whilst on this subject, I may mention that it is most important to carry out the movements of the feet accompanying the exercises exactly as described, and it is advisable to practise them over several times before handling the ball, so as to become accustomed to them, when it will not be necessary to focus the attention on both hands and feet at the same time. Wear gloves or mitts ; they will not only prevent damage to the knuckles, but will give a flatter surface for punching, and you will work with more confidence. A jock-strap is also a desirable item of apparel in this as in all vigorous exercises.

Now, a few hints on practising. If you are a beginner, do not overdo it. Take frequent rests and leave off when you begin to tire, extending the periods as you progress. Clench the fists tightly, and strike the ball with the flat part of the knuckles, back of the hand uppermost. Carelessness in observing these rules is likely to result in knocking up the hands. Never punch the ball downwards as it serves no good purpose, but will surely break the cord, and perhaps tear the loop or the top of the ball. Perform the various punches slowly at first and work up speed as you perfect them. If your punch-ball hangs close to a wall take care not to punch too

## APPARATUS, FIXING, & GENERAL HINTS

vigorously in that direction, or your fist may come in contact with something harder than itself, much to your regret. Practise each exercise until it is thoroughly mastered before proceeding to the next. I know it is a big temptation, and one of the greatest difficulties I have had with pupils has been to keep them from attempting the more advanced exercises before they have learned the preliminary ones, but remember the moral of the hare and tortoise fable, " slow but sure," and you will get there first. Each series of exercises in this book is so arranged that it can be followed through, going from one exercise into the next without a break when proficient in them all, and at each practice it is as well to go through them from the commencement. Practise one arm at a time (except in exercises where both arms have to be used to complete a movement), the left more than the right so that you will eventually be able to use both with equal facility. Should the ball go awry, do not catch hold of it, but watching your opportunity, punch it straight and so get it back to control again. Breathe regularly, inhaling through the nose and filling the lungs until you feel the lower part of the chest expanding. It will be found a great help to practise this when out walking. A good time for exercising is the first thing in the morning, and even if you only put in ten minutes on the ball you will notice what a splendid feeling of fitness you have for the rest of the day. Of course, there is no reason why you should not practise at any other time, and, in fact, after a day's toil a spell at the punching-ball acts like a magic refresher, especially if you are a sedentary worker. Do not, however, practise after a heavy meal, but allow one and a half or two hours to elapse before commencing, otherwise your digestion may be impaired instead of being benefited. Nor should you go to bed immediately after punching the ball. It is advisable, if possible, to take a warm bath after your exercise and finish with a good rub down, using a reliable embrocation in the process.

Finally, remember practice, practice, and more practice is the secret of efficiency. Not necessarily long practices at a stretch, but frequent and regular. Patience and perseverance must be your watchwords.

# CHAPTER I

### PRELIMINARY EXERCISES

The following exercises should be thoroughly learned by all those about to take up ball-punching, whether for boxing, fancy work, or merely as a physical recreation. Lay a solid foundation and the structure you build upon it will be unassailable, but if you scamp the first part of your work you will find the later movements hopelessly difficult, and probably give them up in despair. These you are about to learn are the fundamental punches, so pay particular attention to them.

### EXERCISE No. 1.

*The Straight Punch.*

This is by no means so simple as would at first appear, and the novice will find many pitfalls. He may be following the instructions given below, when he will suddenly discover that his fist has relaxed, or that the ball is going off at a tangent because it is not being hit with the right part of the knuckles, as already described. Then he must set to work again, concentrating on all these points.

Straight Left

Take up a position behind the ball, the toe of the left foot directly in a line with the centre of it, and the right foot at a comfortable distance behind. Raise the left fist ready for striking and the right forearm across the chest. This is, of course, the same attitude as is adopted for sparring, and it will be found that just sufficient room is allowed for the ball to pass the head on the left side. Strike the ball with moderate force perfectly in the centre with the left fist, hitting straight from the shoulder, and following the punch through to the full extent of the arm. Draw the arm back to its original position, and repeat the blow immediately, taking care to fully extend the arm each time, and not forgetting to meet the ball with the first half-way between the swivel and the striking place on the drum of the platform. Beginners will find the rhythm a great help in timing their punches, but it is important to keep the eye on the ball. When you have got this correct in every detail, and can punch the ball perfectly straight—not before—change to the right in the following manner. Meet the ball with a short left-hand punch, i.e., just a jab, not from the shoulder but from the elbow, at the same time reversing the position of the feet by bringing the left back and the right forward, immediately strike the ball with the right fist in the same way as described above for the left. When proficient with the right hand continue changing alternately from left to right and *vice versa*, going through the movements exactly as instructed.

### EXERCISE No. 2.

*Combining Straight Punch and Short Punch.*

Finishing up the previous exercise with a straight left, meet the ball with a short left-hand punch, at the same time bringing the left foot back in line with the right. Now strike the ball with a straight right, swaying the body slightly to the left and follow with a short right. Continue in this way, straight left, short left, straight right, short right. A common fault in this exercise is swaying the body too far, and it is then found impossible to punch straight from the shoulder. It is only necessary to allow just sufficient room for the ball to pass the head.

### EXERCISE No. 3.

*The Tattoo Punch.*

If in difficulties resort to the tattoo punch, is sound advice ; but even apart from this, it is a most useful movement, and occurs more

Tattoo Punch

frequently than any other in the course of these exercises.

Maintaining the same position as in Exercise No. 2, but with the body perfectly upright, follow a short left by bringing the right fist directly over the left in a circular movement, then the left over the right, and continue rotating the fists directly in front of the body. After some practice, move round the ball by taking short paces to the left or right, keeping the ball going as described. In this way confidence will be gained and greater progress made.

## EXERCISE NO. 4.
### *Cross Punches.*

Roll the ball to the left with the tattoo punch, and dropping the left hand slightly, give a short punch across the body with the right fist. Immediately lower the right arm sufficiently to allow the ball to travel to the other side of the drum and meet the ball on the rebound with the left. These punches should come from the elbow, and are directed straight across the body. Whilst practising this exercise, keep your eyes fixed on the swivel and not on the ball, otherwise in turning the head to follow the ball, the body will be shifted and the blows go in the wrong direction.

Cross Punch

## CHAPTER II

### THE PUNCHING-BALL AS A MEANS OF GETTING AND KEEPING FIT

Every athlete knows how easy it is to get out of condition, and how very hard it is to get back again, and yet there are at times circumstances which make it impossible for him to keep up his outdoor training. A long spell of wet weather may keep the runner off the track, the footballer will most probably be handicapped by lack of daylight during his leisure hours and so on, but what can keep him from his daily practice on the punch-ball? It surmounts all these difficulties, and, apart from that, it is a most valuable aid in conjunction with any other mode of training. The following course is designed to promote agility, stimulate the nervous system, quicken the eyesight and at the same time develop the muscles of the shoulders, chest, arms, wrists and legs. Cyclists, scullers, footballers, cricketers, runners, etc., etc., will quickly discover the benefits to be derived from it. So also will the

GETTING AND KEEPING FIT 19

man who has no other motive—and surely there could not be a more worthy one—than to guard the most treasured of possessions, viz., good health and fine physique.

### EXERCISE No. 5.
*Punching Forwards and Backwards.*

Reverting to the tattoo punch, strike the ball with a short left, following immediately with a straight right, at the same time taking a step back so as to be at a full arm's length from the ball. Sway the body slightly to the left, punching the ball backwards as it swings over the right shoulder. As the ball rebounds, step forward immediately, meeting it with a straight right, then a straight left, and stepping back again, punch it over the left shoulder with the right fist. Continue this movement; as speed is worked up it will be necessary to step backwards and forwards very quickly and to keep the arms moving at a very fast rate.

### EXERCISE No. 6.
*Combination of Fists and Elbows.*

Standing with both feet in a line and from 12in. to 18in. apart, give a right-hand cross punch. Drop the arm slightly to allow the

Striking the Ball with the back of the Elbow

ball to travel to the other side of the drum ; immediately raise the elbow to meet it on the rebound, and repeat the movement. After sufficient practice with the right, change to left by bringing the left fist over the right as the ball is struck with the elbow, and, meeting it on the rebound with a cross left, continue as with the right. Change back to the right arm and meet the ball with a left cross on the immediate rebound after striking it with the right elbow ; so that the sequence is right fist, right elbow, left fist. Change to left fist, left elbow, right fist, and subsequently alternate these movements. Next introduce the fists and elbows of both arms in the order right fist, right elbow, left fist, left elbow. In due course a variation may be made by striking the ball two or three times in succession with the same elbow. Having accomplished the foregoing, another punch is introduced. After striking the ball with the right elbow, lower the arm ever so slightly and swing the forearm up and back, meeting the ball with the right fist on the first rebound. In order to strike with the flat part of the knuckles it will be necessary to flick the wrist backwards, and it will at once be seen what a splendid exercise this is for strengthening that particular joint. On the second rebound, catch the ball with a cross

Striking the Ball backwards with the Fist

# GETTING AND KEEPING FIT

left, allowing it to travel to the other side of the drum, then follow with a cross right, repeating the movement as before. Change to left elbow, left fist (backwards), right cross, left cross; then alternately in the following order right cross, right elbow, right fist (backwards), left cross, left elbow, left fist (backwards).

## EXERCISE NO. 7.

### *The Pivot Punch.*

Reverting to the tattoo punch, strike the ball with a straight left, followed by a short left, and at the same time pivot half left on the sole of the foot, bringing the right foot forward. Meet the ball on the immediate rebound with a straight right, and swing completely round with the left arm extended sideways from the shoulder, so that the ball is punched backwards with the left fist. Immediately on regaining the original position follow up with a straight right and a short right; reverse the movement by turning to the right. Put plenty of " vim " behind your punches, swinging round quickly and alternating left and right turns. It will require all your energy, agility, and keen vision.

## Exercise No. 8.

*Pivot Punch, Introducing the Elbows.*

Glance the ball forward into the tattoo punch, then, bringing the right foot forward directly in front of the left, strike the ball with a light straight right-hand punch, at the same time pivoting to the left on the soles of the feet so that the back is towards the ball. Lean slightly forward, and, raising the right elbow backwards, strike the ball with it, turning the body a little from the hips. Meet the second rebound with the left elbow, at the same time bringing the left foot back immediately behind the right, and, pivoting to the left so as to be exactly facing the original position, follow with a straight left. Continue this movement circling right round the ball. After some practice it will not be found difficult to keep the ball going behind the back with alternate elbows for a period, which will greatly benefit the chest and side muscles of the body. A speedier turn round is effected in the following manner : —Following the straight right-hand punch, drop the forearm and meet the ball on the immediate rebound with the outside of the right elbow in turning the body, next striking it with the back of the left elbow and com-

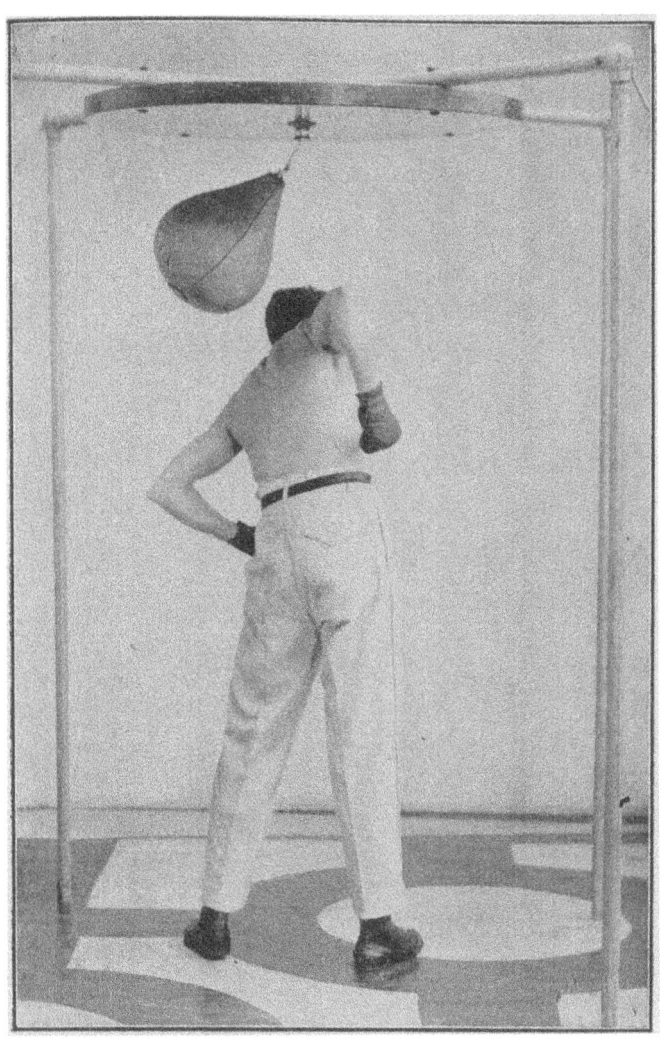

Striking the Ball with the Elbow behind the Body

pleting the turn in the manner already described. Finish with the tattoo punch.

## Exercise No. 9.

### *Tattoo Punch on the Floor Ball.*

For this exercise it is necessary to fasten the ball to the floor or to a batten of wood as is described in a previous part of this book. Some difficulty will be experienced at first in keeping the ball going, and it will be necessary to keep picking it up to restart it, but do not be discouraged. Persevere, taking a rest when tired. Six inches of cord should be allowed for the floor ball, unless otherwise stated. Standing with the feet together and about 7in. behind the ball, throw it forward on to the floor, catching it on the rebound with the right fist and following with the left. Continue with the tattoo punch in the same way as for the suspended ball, taking care to punch straight and perfectly in the centre of the ball. The arms should be stretched downwards as much as possible in order to avoid leaning forward more than is necessary. A frequent mistake when operating the floor ball is to stand with the feet astride. I know this seems a more comfortable position at first, but, as a matter of fact, it is a more

GETTING AND KEEPING FIT 27

tiring one and it hampers freedom of movement. There is also a tendency, which should be strictly avoided, to lower the body in the course of the exercise. After some practice, move round the ball, taking short paces to the left or right, keeping the ball going all the time. Take care to bring the fists directly one over the other and to strike the ball between the swivel and the floor. Unless these instructions are carefully carried out, it will be impossible to keep the ball going for any length of time.

EXERCISE NO. 10.

*Cross Punches on the Floor Ball.*

Now that perfect control has been established with the tattoo punch, roll the ball to the left and give a cross punch with the right. Allow the ball to travel to the right side and meet it on the rebound with a cross left. Continue lefts and rights alternately by a swaying movement of the arms.

EXERCISE NO. 11.

*One-Hand Punch.*

Following a cross right-hand punch, bring the fist back to meet the ball as it rebounds from the right side of the swivel, turning the wrist so as to strike with the flat part of the knuckles. Follow immediately with a cross right and continue. Change to left, commencing with a cross left after the ball has been struck to the right.

## EXERCISE NO. 12.
### *Leg Exercise.*

Following a right-hand cross punch, stand upright, at the same time raising the left knee at right angles to the body, and meet the ball on the rebound from the right side of the swivel with the inside of the foot. Swinging the leg from the knee, meet the rebound from the left with the outside of the foot, and continue in this way. In changing, lower the foot to the ground and strike the ball with a left-hand cross punch, immediately raising the right knee and repeating the movement as with the left. This exercise will test your powers of balance and give the correct poise of body in addition to benefiting the muscles of the leg.

## EXERCISE NO. 13.
### *A Further Leg Exercise.*

Rolling the ball into the tattoo punch, lower the body by bending the knees until almost

Operating Floor Ball with the Feet

sitting on the heels, then continuing the tattoo with the right hand only, place the left on the floor, and lower the body still further to a sitting position, at the same time lifting both feet clear. Immediately strike the ball with the sole of the left foot, following with the right ; continue striking the ball with the soles of the feet, moving them in a rotating manner. In doing this exercise do not rest on the elbows. To rise, place the left hand on the floor and lower the feet, keeping the ball going with the right fist. Gradually raise the body and continue with the double-hand tattoo punch.

## Exercise No. 14.

*Combining Fists and Feet.*

Whilst still continuing the tattoo punch, take an upward jump, lifting both feet clear of the floor, and whilst in the air strike the ball with the sole of the left foot, and on the immediate rebound with the sole of the right. On landing on the feet, resume the double-hand tattoo punch.

## CHAPTER III

### BALL-PUNCHING FOR BOXERS

The punching-ball is used by the boxer with a set purpose and a very definite end ; a special chapter is, therefore, necessary for his requirements. Its first use was by exponents of the noble art, who quickly recognised its sterling merits, and to-day it is second in importance only to the sparring partner in the routine of training. So much depends upon it that the enthusiastic boxer would not dream of using a gymnasium where there was not at least one available for his use. In fact, if he is wise, he will have one at home so that he has a " dumb sparring partner " at his service whenever required. He must, however, avoid all purely fancy work as he would the plague. It is the bane of the boxer. I have done a considerable amount of boxing, and have no reason to be ashamed of my prowess. Nevertheless, I am quite sure that if I had desired to secure the highest honours in this department, I should have been greatly handicapped by having continually practised fancy ball-punching. Still, I have no regrets, for I have had the pleasure of assisting scores of young aspirants by putting them right on the use of the ball, and it has been my privilege to give several champions, including Tommy Burns, Syd. Smith, and Tommy Noble the benefit of my knowledge on this subject. I hope the following instructions in my methods will be of similar benefit to some thousands of others.

Always treat the ball as a living opponent, putting plenty of power behind your punches. Keep your guard up and look to your defence in the same way as you would when actually fighting; for, if you get into the habit of leaving yourself open when punching the ball, it will surely grow upon you, and it is better by far to leave it alone altogether than use it in a lackadaisical manner. Make a practice of having a defence ready for any possible counter every time you make a punch, and never drop both hands to your sides whilst in the course of an exercise. Your arms will, of course, ache to begin with, but it is, first and foremost, to strengthen these members that you are using the ball. Naturally, in a contest the opponents will seize every opportunity to wear down each other's defence, and it will be easy to pick the man who has practised assiduously on the ball, for he will have sufficient strength in his shoulders and arms to withstand all the pressure. I have heard it advocated in some quarters that boxers should stand underneath the ball and strike it with the head backwards and forwards and from side to side, and I, therefore, deem it advisable to utter a word of warning against this. It is said that it develops the muscles of the neck. But what are the facts ? It is an unnatural, jerky movement of the head, which results in a broadening of the neck and a stiffening of the muscles. Is this what the boxer requires ? No, the muscles of his neck should be lithe and supple to enable him to move his head quickly in order to dodge punches, and this condition is attained by the natural movement of the head when slipping the ball, turning the head quickly, etc. Apart from this, such an exercise will result in giving the performer a nasty headache, which will probably become a permanent ailment if the performance is practised often. It is outside the scope of this book to instruct the boxer in footwork, but whilst punching the ball he can practise at the same time all that he has learned in this department. Practices should be of from three to five minutes at a stretch, with one minute intervals.

## JUDGMENT OF DISTANCE.

This is a prime factor in the success or failure of a boxer, for he must have more than an elementary knowledge of exactly when and where to plant his punches in addition to knowing how to deliver them, and there can be no doubt that this is another direction in which the pugilist finds the punching-ball most useful. Judgment of distance for him means nothing so simple as estimating the space between himself and a stationary object, or even a moving one. He may hit the ball ninety-nine times out of a hundred, but if the force of his blows is spent or not fully matured when he actually strikes it, these hits are worthless, and, as a matter of fact, sap the energy of the puncher to a far greater extent than would have been the case if the blows had been well and truly delivered. What, then, is judgment of distance in this sense of the term ? It is gauging to a fraction exactly when and where to hit the ball, so that at the moment of impact the blow is at the height of its speed with the full power of the arm and the weight of the body behind it, whilst perfect balance is maintained. Balance is of course a most important thing, and should receive special consideration.

### Hook Punches.

These are delivered when close to the ball, by sharply bending the elbow and bringing the fist across the body, raising on the toes of the left foot for a left hook or the right foot for a right hook. Keep the other foot quite firm.

### Uppercuts.

With the arm bent, force the fist up, carrying the shoulder forward and raising on to the toes so that the weight of the body adds to the power of the blow. Do not, however, overbalance. In executing these punches, the ball should be struck as it swings backwards.

### Swings.

Stand firmly when delivering these blows. From the sparring attitude, step forward with the right foot, at the same time swinging the right fist on to the ball, giving it all the impetus of the arm and shoulder, but do not carry the body too far forward. Reverse the procedure for a left swing. Never execute these punches wildly, and pay particular attention to defence, because boxers are most apt to leave themselves open in making a blow of this sort.

Half Uppercut

Right Swing

## General Practice.

Adopt the proper sparring attitude, left foot forward, left shoulder well up and chin drawn in, right forearm across the chest and left fist at about the height of the chin. Keep the fists moving continually. Start off with the left lead as described in Exercise No. 1 of this book. After striking the ball, take two short steps backwards, right foot first, and allow the ball to rebound several times. Then step in and again repeat the blow. When stepping back, take care not to carry the left foot behind the right, otherwise the balance will be upset. Work up speed and power of punch as you proceed, and move round the ball. Change to the right lead in the manner described, and then alternate the punches, stepping briskly in and out, moving to right and left, blocking, slipping, dodging, etc. Then follow a quick succession of left leads by hooking the right as powerfully as possible, and follow with a straight left. Your eyesight will have to be very keen before you can get in a perfect left on the ball without letting it first rebound quite a number of times after that hook. Then, of course, the left hook is practised. Now introduce left and right half, or jab, uppercuts. It is not advisable to execute a full uppercut on the punching-ball as, if correctly done, it is dangerous for the hands, and if incorrectly done may as well be left alone. Wait until sparring with a partner, therefore, before attempting it. Finish by varying all the blows and fighting the ball as you would an actual opponent in a contest, occasionally feinting with left or right, shifting the position and landing with the other fist. It is as well to have a ball fastened to the wall, waist-high, directly under the platform ball, and whilst fighting the suspended ball, step right in now and again, and lifting the wall ball, give it a few vigorous cross punches. Then step back and continue with the suspended ball immediately. There is no finer exercise than this for in-fighting practice. Exercise No. 13 in Chapter II should be carried out to give suppleness to the muscles of the legs.

Whilst the swing ball is indispensable to the boxer, the double-ended pattern should also be used in conjunction with it if possible, because it has one important advantage. That is, that the line of its return is less certain and more varied, so that the manipulator has to punch at every possible angle and to think quickly in doing it.

## CHAPTER IV

### FANCY BALL-PUNCHING

He who aspires to become an expert in the more intricate movements of this art must be prepared to spend unlimited time at practice, for, although they look quite simple when performed, it will only be necessary to try them to find out how difficult they really are. I suppose I have a natural aptitude for ball-punching, but notwithstanding this, I have had to keep at it, never missing a day's practice, in order to attain absolute proficiency and even now I do not claim to know all there is to know about it, because its possibilities are limitless. The movements hereafter described are mostly of my own origination, and several of them I have never to this day seen any other ball-puncher, amateur or professional, perform. Of course, this chapter by no means exhausts the variety of combinations that can be made, and it is for the enthusiast to think out others for himself. In fact, that is half the joy of fancy

FANCY BALL-PUNCHING 41

ball-punching, and, then again, in public exhibitions originality counts more than anything else.

In the first place, it is necessary to have mastered all the exercises in Chapters I and II, and to have absolute confidence that you can go through them without " bungling " anywhere. Then and then only should the following movements be learned, and the whole series be run through without a break.

A COMBINATION OF FISTS AND ELBOWS.

This is an extension of Exercise No. 6 and should follow it. After striking the ball with the right elbow, meet it on the rebound with a left-hand cross punch under the right arm, following with the right elbow and then the left fist over the right arm. Only just raise or lower the elbow as much as is necessary to allow the ball to be struck in the centre with the left fist. Continue this, occasionally allowing the ball to travel to the other side of the drum and introducing a right cross. Change to left and then use both arms alternately. A further extension of this movement is made by bringing the fist back on to the ball after it has been struck by the elbow for the second time ; follow immediately with a cross punch with the other fist. Practice this with right only at first, then left, and then alternately. Vary by striking the ball two or three times in succession with the elbow and fist of the same arm.

## THE DOUBLE PUNCH.

Another combination of fists and elbows, which is very spectacular when properly carried out and which makes the ball travel at an exceedingly fast rate with a minimum of energy, is executed as follows : – Strike the ball with a right-hand cross punch, dropping the fist and meeting the immediate rebound with the outside of the right elbow. Follow the punch through so that the ball is able to travel to the other side of the drum ; immediately bring the elbow back to meet it on the first rebound and the fist on the second. When proficient with the right, change to left and subsequently alternate both arms. The sequence then is : Right cross, right elbow (outside), right elbow (back), right fist (backwards), left cross, left elbow (outside), left elbow (back), left fist (backwards).

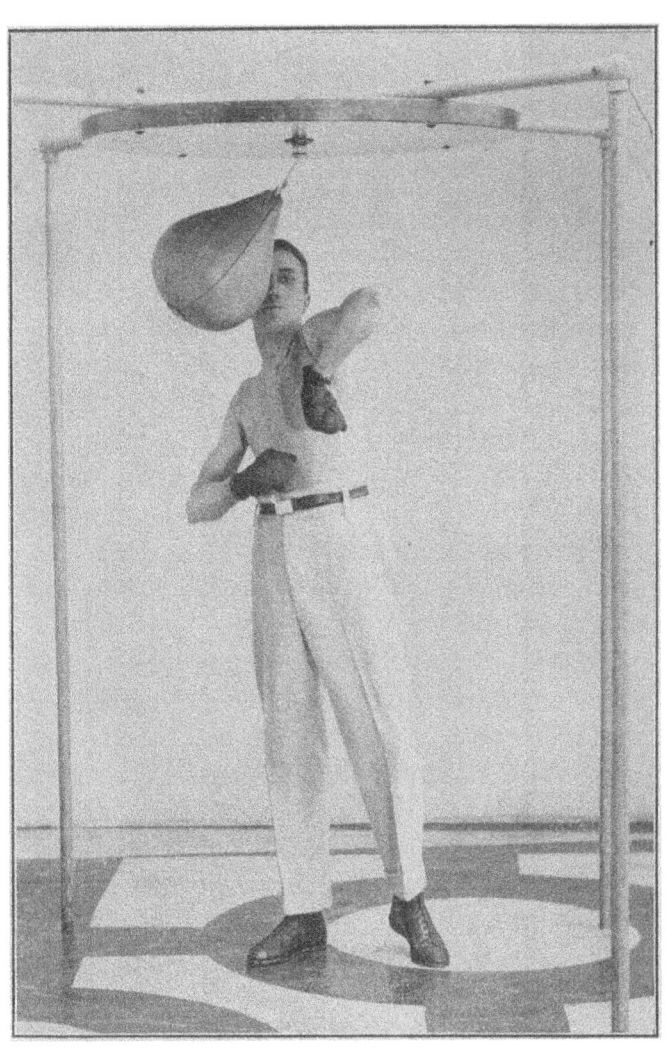

Striking the Ball with the Outside of the Elbow

## Operating Two Platform Balls at the Same Time.

Fix two balls about 2ft. apart. Standing between them and not too far back, raise both arms level with the balls and start them simultaneously with single-hand tattoo punches straight to the front. Glance them half-way to the left; turning the body slightly from the hips and lowering the right fist, strike the right ball with the outside of the elbow, at the same time as the left-hand ball is struck with the left fist and in the same direction; meet the rebounds with the outside of the left elbow and the right fist. After repeating this several times, allow the balls to swing to the left, and strike them on the rebounds with the right fist and the back of the left elbow, and then to the right with the left fist and the back of the right elbow. Drawing both arms back, revert to tattoo punches straight to the front, then allowing the balls to pass over the arms, bring the elbows back to meet them on the rebounds, and continue. Take a short step backwards and punch both balls vigorously, bringing the fists back on to them immediately. This is a good rally to finish up with.

Operating two Platform Balls at the same time

## Operating Three Platform Balls at the Same Time.

Fix a third ball exactly between the other two, and starting the outside balls off with tattoo punches, as in the previous movement, tap the third ball with the top of the forehead, bending the head slightly forward. This is the only movement that can be effected with three platform balls, but when properly carried out is evidence of considerable skill and well worth inclusion in any exhibition. The secret of its accomplishment is to keep the head and fists going together, and to avoid moving the head up and down. All three balls must be struck perfectly in the centre so as to keep them dead straight.

## The Wall Ball.

Fix the swivel to the wall waist high, or if a four-poster platform is used a board of sufficient size can be secured between two of the uprights. Two inches of cord only should be allowed. Stand with the feet in a line and at a comfortable distance apart, sufficiently behind the ball to allow perfect freedom of movement for the arms. Lift the ball and commence with a double-hand tattoo punch in a downward direction, then striking the ball with a right of sufficient force to carry it over the swivel, continue the same punch but in an upward direction. Practice this, continually changing from downwards to upwards punching and *vice versa*.

PUNCHING THE BALL ROUND A CIRCLE.

Having established a firm control over the ball with the tattoo punch, start from directly under the swivel and gradually work right round the drum, moving the body sufficiently to face the direction in which the ball is being punched. No small amount of practice will be necessary before the complete circle can be made without the ball dropping, and it will have to be punched vigorously all the time.

COMBINING STRAIGHT AND SHORT PUNCHES.

Reverting to the downwards tattoo punch, strike the ball with a straight right of sufficient force to carry it over the swivel and back again, meeting it with a short right-hand punch from the elbow on the second rebound. Repeat with the left hand and continue with alternate lefts and rights.

CROSS PUNCHES.

Next bring the ball to a horizontal position on the left with the tattoo punch, then striking it with a hard right straight across the body, follow with the left in a similar manner, meeting the ball on the rebound from the other side of the swivel. Continue with alternate lefts and rights in this way. It will be found that the ball has a tendency to drop, which can only be overcome by perfect accuracy of punching, and as the ensuing movements all depend on this, it is worth while to spend some time upon it.

### COMBINATIONS OF ELBOWS AND FISTS.

Following a right cross, strike the ball on the immediate rebound with the outside of the right elbow, then allowing the ball to travel to the other side repeat with the left arm. The next movement is similar, but the ball is allowed to go to the right immediately after it has been struck with the right fist, and the elbow is brought back to meet the rebound from that side. The left, of course, is then used in the same way. These two movements may be combined, and a backwards punch with the fist introduced after the ball has been struck by the elbow, in this order : Right fist, right elbow (outside), right elbow (back), right fist (backwards), left fist, left elbow (outside), left elbow (back), left fist (backwards). This

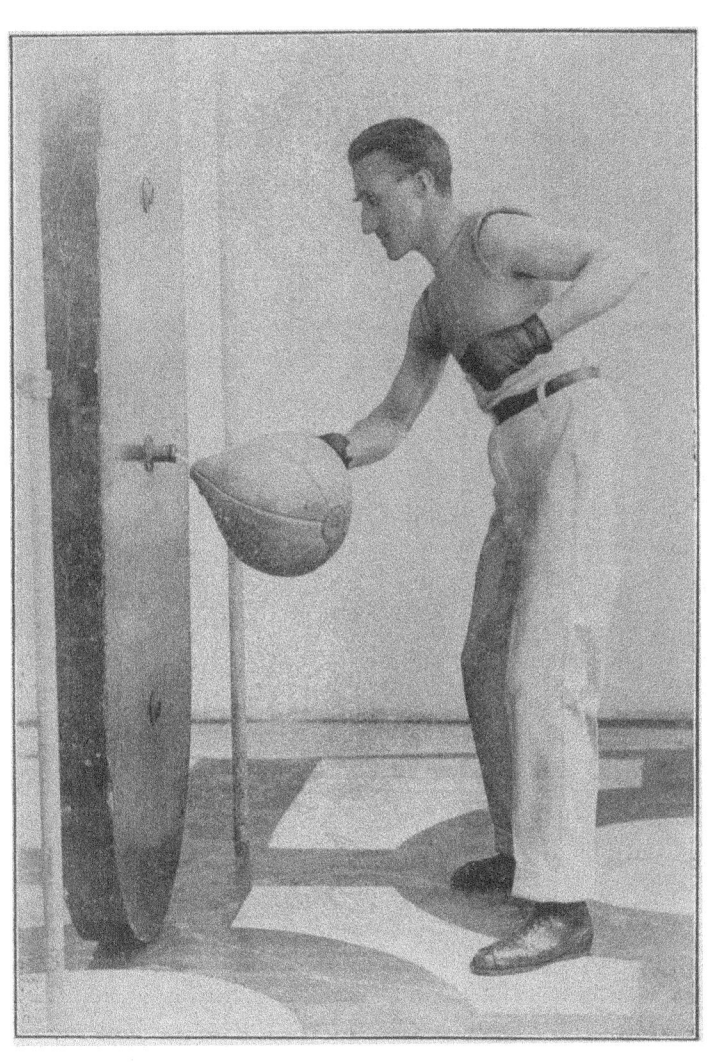

Cross Punch on the Wall Ball

movement is further extended as follows: After the ball has been struck to the right with the right elbow, raise the arm and cross the left fist under it, to catch the immediate rebound. Then strike the ball again with the back of the right elbow and bring the right fist back on to it as in the previous movement. Repeat with the left and then alternate left and right arms. Vary the movement by striking the ball two or three times in succession with the right elbow and left fist on the right side, and the left elbow and right fist on the left side. When competently performed, this is dazzling to the onlooker, so fast does the ball move.

## THE PIVOT PUNCH.

Revert to straight cross punches, and simultaneously with a right cross, pivot round on the sole of the left foot so as to be facing the other way. Meet the ball on the rebound from the other side of the swivel with the right elbow by bringing it across the back of the body, then the left elbow in a similar manner, at the same time pivoting back to the original position and completing the movement with a left cross. Vary this by keeping the ball going with the elbows behind the back, for a short period.

## FANCY BALL-PUNCHING

### The Floor Ball.

Exercises Nos. 9 to 14 should, of course, have been thoroughly mastered before the following movements are attempted, as they are all part of the fancy ball-puncher's repertoire. Extend Exercise No. 10 by introducing a left cross after the ball has been struck to the right by the right fist, and a right cross after it has been struck to the left with the left fist. Then alternate the double punch with each hand, that is, striking the ball to the left and right with the right fist, then to the right and left with the left fist.

### Combinations of Fists and Elbows.

Do not lower the body in the course of the following movements, but when the ball is being struck with the right elbow, drop the right shoulder and the same with the left. Reverting to the cross punch, lift the fist immediately after giving a right cross and meet the rebound from the other side of the swivel with the back of the elbow. Repeat with the left, and then alternate rights and lefts. Follow this with the combination of right fist, right elbow, right fist, by dropping the fist on to the ball immediately after it has been struck with the right elbow; then

Fist and Elbow Punch on the Floor Ball

repeat with the left fist, left elbow, and left fist. Alternate fists and elbows. By shortening the cord of the ball to 2in., all the foregoing movements can be executed in a kneeling position. The pivot punch can be carried out in exactly the same manner on the floor ball as on the wall ball, but the ball is struck with the fists behind the back instead of the elbows.

### OPERATING THE BALL WITH THE KNEES.

For this purpose, the cord should be of sufficient length to allow the centre of the ball to reach to the knee. Draw the feet up to the swivel, so that it is between the toes, and, lifting the ball, throw it forward, catching it on the rebound with the left knee, and on the subsequent rebound with the right knee. Take care not to open the knees outwards or the ball will go awry; and do not bend the knees forward too much. Just raising the heels $1\frac{1}{4}$in. off the floor will be found to be sufficient. Move round by turning slightly on the soles of the feet, keeping the ball going all the time. Then, taking a step back, carry on with the double-hand tattoo punch, and rolling the ball to the left, finish with a rally on the cross punch.

## Operating Two Floor Balls Simultaneously.

Fix two balls to the floor 2ft. apart, and start them off with single-hand tattoo punches, then rolling them both to the left, hit with sufficient force to carry them to the right side of the swivel. Meet them on the rebound, the right-hand ball with the back of the right elbow, and the left-hand ball with the left fist. Let them travel to the left and meet the left-hand ball with the back of the left elbow and the right-hand ball with the right fist. Continue in this way. Revert to the forward tattoo punches, and stepping a little closer to the balls, punch them backwards and forwards, turning the wrists so that the flat part of the knuckles is used each time. For the following movement, bring the swivels closer together, allowing only sufficient room for both feet to be inserted between them. The cord of both balls should be sufficiently long to allow them to reach to the knees. Standing with the feet together, between the swivels, lift both balls and start them with single-hand tattoo punches in a slightly oblique direction. When they are well under control, stand upright, and bending the knees forward and slightly outwards, keep the balls going in this manner. It is as well to practise the movement with the knees without operating the balls at first, as it is most important that they should be bent in the same direction every time.

Two floor balls can also be operated whilst lying flat on the back in the following manner. Fasten two balls so that when lying down one is 2in. from the head and the other 1in. from the feet. Lie flat on the back, and lifting the latter ball between the feet, commence a tattoo upon it with the soles of both feet, moving them with a circular motion. Practise this ball alone at first, and should it fall to the floor, do not raise the body but lift it with the feet again. When it can be kept going without difficulty, lift the other ball by the neck with one hand and set it going with the double-hand tattoo punch over the top of the head. The two balls will thus be in motion at the same time.

## Operating Three Floor Balls Simultaneously.

Fix two balls about 18in. behind a third and about 2ft. 4in. apart, forming an isosceles triangle. These measurements are, however,

Operating Three Floor Balls Simultaneously

only approximate and will, of course, have to be varied according to the height, etc., of the operator. The best means of ascertaining the required distance is to commence with the measurements given above and to alter them, if necessary, to suit individual requirements after a trial has been made. The length of cord for each ball in this instance should be 2in. Place the side balls behind their swivels so that they will not be in the way, then starting the front ball with the tattoo punch go through the movements as described in Exercise No. 13. When this ball is well under control with the feet, lift both side balls and start them simultaneously with tattoo punches in an oblique direction. Unless all three balls are kept in time it will not be possible to keep them going, and this is where difficulty will be met with at first; but practice will soon overcome it. It is quite likely that cramp will attack the thighs almost as soon as this movement is started; if this occurs, rest immediately, but do not give up altogether as the tendency will disappear after a time. No variety can be added to this movement, but it is very spectacular when carried through perfectly. To finish, let the side balls drop and raise the body to the feet as described in Exercise No. 13.

## Operating Four Floor Balls Simultaneously.

Fix two balls about 7in. apart and another two 10in. in front and about 5in. apart. The length of cord for each ball must be the same, i.e., sufficient to allow the centre of the ball to reach to the knees. Commence with the rear balls as in the third movement for operating two floor balls, and stooping very gradually lift the front balls and set them in motion with tattoo punches straight to the front. If the rear balls begin to slack it will, no doubt, be due to opening the knees too wide. Pay attention to this and complete control will soon be gained.

## Operating Two Platform Balls and Two Floor Balls Simultaneously.

Standing 6in. behind the suspended balls, with the feet together and the floor balls one on each side of them, operate the latter with the knees as described in the previous paragraph. Then, raising both arms to the height of the shoulders, strike the platform balls directly forwards with tattoo punches. By combining the movement described on Page 46 with the two floor balls, five balls can be kept in motion at the same time.

Operating Two Suspended Balls and Two Floor Balls Simultaneously

## Operating Platform, Wall and Floor Balls Simultaneously.

The ball fastened to the wall should be in line with the platform ball, and the floor ball should be 6in. behind them. Standing with the feet one on each side of the swivel, commence by operating the floor ball with the knees as described on Page 53. When this is well under control, set the wall ball going with a single-hand tattoo punch in a horizontal direction, and finally the platform ball with the other hand. Practise each ball separately at first, then two together before trying all three simultaneously.

## Punching the Ball to Music.

This needs some practice, but it is well worth it as it is both amusing and entertaining, and should be included in any exhibition. Get one of your musical friends to play an instrument whilst you are punching the ball, and try to pick up the rhythm as you proceed. Lively tunes are best to start with, and the tattoo on fists and elbows will come in very useful here; but after a time you will be able to accompany almost any tune and at the same time introduce a good variety of punches. It is also possible to get the rhythm of a given tune without the accompaniment of a musical instrument, and rap it out so that it will be easily recognised.

Operating Three Balls Simultaneously

# CHAPTER V

### THE DOUBLE-ENDED PUNCH-BALL.

It is often complained that this type of ball is monotonous, and that when using it only straightforward punching can be engaged in, interest in consequence soon being lost. Whilst, compared with the swing ball, its possibilities are somewhat limited, there are, however, a variety of punches which may be practised on it. As a matter of fact, I have at times given exhibitions in public on this ball alone, with complete success. Some of the movements I give below, others you will find out for yourself, and for this very reason will practise them with more zest. In selecting a ball of this pattern, see that the strength of the springs accords with your own punching power, and that the fittings are strong without being heavy enough to tear away from the case. One with metal swivels for attaching the springs to the ball is best, because it can then revolve without twisting the rubbers or

## THE DOUBLE-ENDED PUNCH-BALL

straps, with a consequent saving of wear and tear. Do not inflate it to its utmost limit, and do not overstretch the springs. I do not know why, but nine people out of ten using a fixed punch-ball think that it is more efficacious when blown out as hard as a football and the springs stretched until there is no elasticity left in them. It is obviously not so; yet frequently I am asked to investigate the cause of faulty action in a ball of this kind, and I almost invariably trace it to these two reasons. On the other hand, the ball should not, of course, be flabby, or the seams of the case will rub the bladder and cause trouble in that way. Slip the top ring on the ceiling hook, and if by taking the bottom one with the thumb and forefinger of one hand it can just be stretched to the bottom hook, it will be sufficiently taut. Do not, under any circumstances, take hold of the ball itself when performing this operation. The distance between the hooks should be from 8ft. to 12ft. Adjust the straps or cords so that the ball is in line with the shoulders. Always punch it in the centre with the flat part of the knuckles, palms turned downwards. Meet the ball with the fist as it comes towards you, and move backwards and forwards according to the strength of your blows.

## Tattoo and Straight Punches.

Standing with the left foot forward in line with the ball and with the fists in attitude for sparring, commence a tattoo punch with the left fist, catching the ball on every rebound, taking care to punch the ball straight to the front. Change to right by giving the ball a short jab with the left fist and at the same time bringing the left foot back and the right forward. Then bring the left foot up in line with the right, and continue with a double-hand tattoo punch. Revert to the first position, but step a little further back and strike the ball with a straight left, putting full force behind the blow. Miss the first rebound and repeat the punch on the second. Practise this, and then change to right in the same manner as for the tattoo punch. Alternate lefts and rights, changing the position of the feet with each blow, intervening the straight punches with short jabs, thus  Straight left, short left, straight right, short right.


## Fists and Elbows.

Maintaining the same position as for the straight left, strike the ball with the left fist, and immediately bring the forearm across the

Straight Left on Double-ended Ball

body. Miss the first rebound, and leaning slightly forward, catch the ball on the second with the front of the left elbow. Repeat this several times, then change to right as previously described, and subsequently alternate lefts and rights. By striking the ball only on every other rebound, it is possible to put more power behind the blows.

## Hook Punches.

With both feet in a line, strike the ball with a left hook punch, which will cause it to travel in a circle, and as it comes round meet it with a right hook. As the left fist strikes the ball, turn slightly on the sole of the left foot, keeping the right quite firm, and *vice versa* for the right hook. This will enable you to put the weight of the body behind the blow without over-balancing. Combine a straight left and right hook and a straight right and left hook. Two or three straight punches should precede each hook, and the position of the feet should be changed only when going from straight left to straight right or *vice versa*. Bringing the feet in line again, strike the ball with a left hook, and bring the left elbow back on to it as it comes round. Practise this with both left

THE DOUBLE-ENDED PUNCH-BALL 67

and right arms. Repeat the movement, but instead of bringing the elbow back on to the ball, strike it with the outside of the other elbow, left hook, right elbow, left hook, right hook, left elbow, right hook, and so on.

PIVOT PUNCHES.

Repeat the right hook, and at the same time face about by pivoting on the sole of the left foot. Then catch the ball with the back of the right elbow as it comes round behind the body, following with the left elbow in a similar manner, and pivoting back to the original position, catch the ball with a left hook. Step back, punching the ball out as far as possible with straight lefts, then swing round on the sole of the left foot, extend the right arm outwards from the shoulder, and strike the ball backwards with the left fist. Immediately complete the turn, and follow with a straight right. Reverse the movement, turning to the right.

THE CANE STEM PUNCH-BALL.

This type of ball is very useful for developing punching power, but is rather apt to make one slow if practised on often, and for this reason it is not so popular as either the swing or the double-ended patterns. They are, however, frequently found in gymnasiums, and where it is not convenient to fix either of the others. Various patterns are to be had, some with a heavy iron base, and others with a flange which screws to the floor. The latter is preferable, because it cannot get in the way when stepping in and out or moving round the ball. The cane should be adjustable so that it can be heightened or lowered to suit persons of different heights. The centre of the ball should be in line with the chin. The spring should be strong, closely wound, and not sharply bent where it connects with the base and the cane, otherwise it will snap on the slightest provocation, especially in cold weather. Do not bend the ball backwards or forwards to start it; commence by punching it straight forward. When moving backwards the hands will have to be lowered. Keep your eyes fixed on the ball, and be sure to hit it fairly in the centre, otherwise you are likely to strike the cane or metal fittings and so damage your knuckles. The same exercises should be practised on this as on the double-ended ball, but there are two additions which can only be carried out on this ball, and will be found very useful. The first is to strike the ball with a straight left, and as it returns lift the left knee to meet it ; follow with a straight right and the right knee. The second is to punch the ball as hard as possible with straight lefts, then, watching your opportunity, lie flat on your back on the ground, and keep it going with the feet. This is a splendid exercise for the legs.

A Selection Of Classic Instructive Titles
Relating To The Art Of Pugilism & Self Defence
In Both War & Peace
Find our entire selection
@ naval-military-press.com


ALL-IN FIGHTING

The distilled knowledge of W.E. Fairbairn, legendary SOE instructor in unarmed combat, and inventor of the Sykes-Fairbairn knife, who learned his deadly skills in 30 years on the Shanghai waterfront. Fully illustrated.
9781847348531


ART OF BOXING AND SCIENCE OF SELF DEFENCE

Former Lightweight Champion Billy Edwards shares the techniques and strategies of the sweet science in his beautifully illustrated boxing guide. Explore boxing's transition from bare knuckle spectacle to today's Marquis of Queensbury ruleset.
9781474539548

## SELF DEFENCE OR THE ART OF BOXING

Ned Donnelly was a pioneer of boxing training during the late Victorian era. Explore the strategies and techniques used by this trainer of champions via a series of easy-to-follow illustrations and clear, concise coaching steps.

9781474539562

## JACK GOODWIN'S BOXING

This 1920's boxing masterpiece by Jack Goodwin puts you in the shoes of a coach in that era. Uncover the best ways to run, manage and train boxers as taught by Jack Goodwin, a champion and trainer of champions in the noble science.

9781474539586

## THE COMPLETE BOXER

Gunner Moir provides detailed instructions on the techniques he deployed to become British Heavyweight Champion. Taught in a series of easy to learn techniques, combinations, and boxing strategies.

9781474539609

## ART OF WRESTLING
George de Relwyskow Army Gymnastic Staff

In the appreciation to this book Captain Daniels, V.C., M.C., Rifle Brigade, states: "In adding a word to this book on the style of wrestling as taught at the Headquarters Gymnasium of the British Army, and having had personal experience in the various holds and throws taught, I consider it has been of great value in the training of the soldier, and the bringing out of those qualities of grit and determination which have been seen in all ranks who have taken an active part throughout the greatest war in history." 1919.

9781783313563

## KILL OR GET KILLED

Rex Applegate's "kill or be killed" helped prepare America's marines, soldiers, sailors, spies and airmen for the realities of war. This highly shared and respected work provides all you need to know about unarmed combat and close quarter engagement with the enemy.

9781474539661

### BOXING (V-Five)
The Aviation Training Office of the Chief of Naval Operations
The game-changing V-Five suite of training manuals helped get a generation of American aviators fit for war. Here we explore how the airmen of the US navy trained in boxing as part of their military fitness regime.
9781474539623

### THE TEXTBOOK OF WRESTLING
Get your wrestling skills matt-ready from wrestling champion and world-renown trainer Ernest Gruhn. Replete with detailed holds, throws, pins and strategies for success in a wide range of wrestling rulesets.
9781474539647

### MANUAL OF PHYSICAL TRAINING 1914
(United States Army)
Published just prior to the outbreak of World War 1, this beautifully illustrated guide was designed to revolutionise the combat fitness and readiness of the US Army covering a wide range of gymnastic and combat calisthenic exercises.
9781474539708

### DEAL THE FIRST DEADLY BLOW
United States Department of the Army
This Vietnam-era classic showcases in detail how the US Forces trained in close quarter combat. Known as the "encyclopaedia of combat" it helped a generation learn how to become devastating effective with empty hands, knives and bayonets alike.
9781474539722

HAND-TO-HAND COMBAT
Bureau of Aeronautics U.S Navy 1943

This is one of the best combative manuals from World War 2, developed by the US Navy V-Five Staff, that included the renowned American wrestler Wesley Brown. It is then not especially surprising that wrestling skills predominate in this manual, and form the base skill-set for this combative system.

9781474537391

ABWEHR ENGLISCHER GANGSTER METHODEN DEFENSE OF ENGLISH GANGSTERS METHODS – SILENT KILLING – FULL ENGLISH TRANSLATION

In 1942 the Wehrmacht published a training manual with the goal of countering the "silent killing" tactics used by the British commando units. The manual was – much in line with typical National Socialist terminology –titled "Abwehr Englischer Gangster-methoden" or "Defence Against English Gangster methods".

This book was compiled due the Wehrmacht intelligence operatives uncovering of a British hand-to-hand course for the SOE, Commandos, et al, on methods of quick and silent killing (undoubtedly developed by W. E. Fairbairn and E. A. Sykes). They correctly assessed that their troops in general and particularly the Geheime Staatspolizei (Gestapo), Sicherheitsdienst (SD), their security guards, and sentries would be in grave danger when confronted by men trained in these methods. This manual/program was the Wehrmacht's response.

9781474538336

## BOXING FOR BOYS

Regtl. Sergt.-Major E & B Dent Army Gymnastic Headquarters
A successful system of boxing instruction for large classes, to allow tuition with no detriment to the "backward or shy pupil". Covers Kit-On, Guard-Sparring-Advance-Point & Mark-Ducking-Medicine, Bag-Left & Right Hooks etc. The author considered that boxing systematically taught to the youth was beneficial exercise, and would have a marked elevating influence on the national character.
9781783314607

## HAND-TO-HAND FIGHTING

A System Of Personal Defence For The Soldier (1918)
A tough book on the art of hand to hand fighting in the trenches of the Great War. Demonstrating techniques utilised to "do away with the enemy", many of which are barred in clean wrestling, the book includes good clear photographic illustrations presenting important attack methods including the "Hammer Lock", "Kidney Kick", "Head Twist", "Knee Groin Kick", and the "Knee Break", all very important in a man to man, life or death encounter, when fighting in the mud of the trenches.
9781783313983

## HAND TO HAND COMBAT

Francois d'Eliscu taught thousands of U.S. Army Rangers how to fight down and dirty in World War II. d'Eliscu doesn't get the press that Fairbairn and Applegate do, but he did a commendable job writing this book. It is basic, meant for training raw recruits in a short amount of time before sending them to the front, but simple is good when you are in combat, as most combative experts' will tell you.

9781474535823

## COLD STEEL

A cold-war combatives classic. John Styers, US Marine and WW2 veteran, lays out his approach to close quarters combat with rifle, bayonet, stick, knife and empty hands. Explore what helped wartime and post-war Marines stay ahead of the competition with lucid imagery and clear combative descriptions.

9781474540643

## THE COMPLETE KANO JIU-JITSU

Join world-famous physical culture expert H. Irving Hancock, and Jiu-Jitsu specialist Katsukama Higashi as they showcase the art of 'Kano Jiu-Jitsu' now known as Judo. Get an exclusive glimpse into the transitional era of the martial art, alongside how it uses Japanese physical culture methodologies for self-improvement.

9781474540735

WE Fairbairn's Complete Compendium of Lethal, Unarmed, Hand-to-Hand Combat Methods and Fighting In Colour
All 844 images of Fairbairn and his assistants can now for the first time be seen in full colour, lending a clarity to the practical methods of mastering the manner of dealing with an assailant, both in time of war and when placed in difficulty during unpleasant modern urban situations. These various holds, trips, kicks, blows etc. allow the average man or woman a position of security against almost any form of armed or unarmed attack.

Captain W.E. Fairbairn would have approved of this new colour version, that gives an illustrative clarity to the original that was lacking in previous monochrome reprints of his work.

All six of W.E. Fairbairn's works in one binding to create the ultimate colour compendium: Get Tough-All-In Fighting-Shooting to Live-Scientific Self-Defence-Hands Off!-Defend
9781783318735

## SELF DEFENCE FOR WOMEN COMBATO

Join the Canadian combatives legend William "Bill" Underwood as he showcases self-defence for women. Over the course of clear photography, sketches and instructions he

lays out a curriculum for self-defence for the attacks women would be most likely to face.
9781474540711

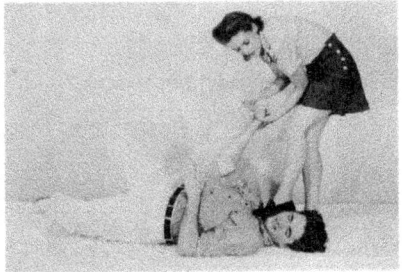

## SCIENTIFIC UNARMED COMBAT
### The Art of Dynamic Self-Defence

Learn the esoteric Sri Lankan art of 'Cheena-Adi' with R. A Vairamuttu. This guide explores armed and unarmed self-defence drawing heavily from Indian martial culture, alongside wellness and development from Indian physical culture, fitness, diet and medicine.

9781474540728

## THE NEW SCIENCE
### Weaponless Defence

Join wrestling champions Prof F. S Lewis, William V Gregory and Boxing Champ Tommy Burns as they showcase street orientated self-defence from people with a proven track record of fighting success. This 1906 manual via a series of photos and instructions lays out simple, tried and tested ways to keep yourself safe.

9781474540704

## COMBAT CONDITIONING MANUAL
### Jiu-Jitsu Defence, Bayonet Defence and Club Defence

This 1942 guide for marines lays out the basics of combat Ju Jitsu as part of an overall training regimen for US Marines. It's a holistic guide that covers defences against armed and unarmed attackers, physical fitness and even first aid.

9781474540698

### BOXING TAUGHT THROUGH "SLOW MOTION FILM"

Learn the ropes from the best fighters of the 1900s-1930s in this unique boxing manual. Using stills from super slow-mo fight footage, this treasure trove unpacks the skills, tips and tactics of the champs for you to emulate at home.

9781474540681

### HOW TO BOX CORRECTLY

Explore the art of boxing according to famous Bronx boxing brand Ben Lee in this 1944 how-to guide. Learn the ropes from one of the nation's top trainers and boxing journalists John J. Romano, in this warmly illustrated guide to the sweet science.

9781474540674

### THE ART OF IN-FIGHTING BY FRANK KLAUS

German-American Middleweight Champ Frank Klaus showcases his KO-scoring boxing IQ in this 1913 guide. Containing clear and easy to understand photography and descriptions, Klaus gives us an insight into the emerging hard-hitting American style of professional boxing.

9781474541473

### THE ART OF BOXING AND HINTS ON TRAINING
Crafted just after WW1 in 1919, this guide by Royal Naval Physical Training, Chief Staff Instructor J.O'Neil explores the military benefits of boxing. Showcasing via lucid text and full page photography.
9781474541510

### JIM DRISCOLL'S TEXTBOOK OF BOXING
Driscoll was a former Featherweight World Champion and in this 1914 guide, he uses cutting edge and clear photography to showcase the new scientific boxing method. Driscoll showcases to the audience the way to best combine British and American boxing training and fighting philosophy.
9781474541466

### JUDO AND ITS USE IN HAND TO HAND COMBAT FROM SEABEES NAVAL ENGINEERING CORPS
Brought to you by William Caldwell of the Seabees Naval Engineering Corps. This WW2 close combat classic provides an insight into the "Combat Judo" used by the navy to prepare personnel for the dangers of theatre. Fully photographed and accessible with clear instructional content to follow.
9781474541480

### AMERICAN JUDO ILLUSTRATED
Brought to you by William Caldwell of the Seabees Naval Engineering Corps. This WW2 close combat classic provides an insight into the "Combat Judo" used by the navy to prepare personnel for the dangers of theatre. Fully photographed and accessible with clear instructional content to follow.
9781474541527

## HAND TO HAND COMBAT - Field Manual 21-150

An example of Cold War / Korean War close combat training. Filled with instructor notes and clear imagery covering unarmed and "cold weapon" combat such as bayonet, knife and garrotte.

9781474541459

## BOXING

This 1906 guide from former English Heavyweight Champion Captain Johnstone, showcases the leading techniques, skills, strategies and fighting philosophies of the day. Brought to life with vivid storytelling from military boxing advocates alongside lucid photography and crisp follow-along guidance for boxers to follow.

9781474541534

## KILL OR GET KILLED

Lt Col. Rex Applegate's WW2 Combat Classic 'Kill or Get Killed' is one of the most detailed and comprehensive guides of armed and unarmed combat ever written. From unarmed, to knife, bayonet, pistol, garotte and more – Applegate provides written descriptions, photographs, illustrations on more to showcase and share the skills of forces like the O.S.S.

9781474541541

## BALL PUNCHING - A PICTORIAL GUIDE TO THE SPEEDBAG

This 1922 guide from Tom Carpenter is a response to the 'speedbag' craze of the early part of the century. It showcases via clear instructions and photography how to best use tools such as maize, speed and double-end bags for fitness and fighting skills.

9781474541503

SCIENTIFIC BOXING FROM A FISTIC EXPERT
Diet - Fight Training - K.O. Punching
This 1937 guide to the American school and style of professional boxing provides a clear and well-illustrated suite of technical skills and drills to compete successfully. Replete with training advice, rule guidance and ring Generalship principles to help boxers be inline with the latest advice and training acumen.
9781474541497

www.ingramcontent.com/pod-product-compliance
Lightning Source LLC
LaVergne TN
LVHW010319070426
835510LV00031B/3452